Women in Conservation

Jane Goodall

Chimpanzee Protector

Robin S. Doak

Heinemann
LIBRARY

Chicago, Illinois

Edited by Clare Lewis, Abby Colich, Diyan Leake, and Gina Kammer
Designed by Philippa Jenkins
Original illustrations © Capstone Global Library Ltd 2014
Illustrated by Oxford Designers and Illustrators p12, HL Studios p15
Picture research by Tracy Cummins
Production by Victoria Fitzgerald
Originated by Capstone Global Library Ltd
Printed and bound in China by CTPS

Library of Congress Cataloging-in-Publication Data

ISBN 978-1-4846-0469-4 (hardcover)
ISBN 978-1-4846-0474-8 (paperback)
ISBN 978-1-4846-0484-7 (eBook PDF)

18 17 16 15 14
10 9 8 7 6 5 4 3 2 1

Acknowledgments
We would like to thank the following for permission to reproduce photographs: Alamy: © Everett Collection Inc, 28; Corbis: © Bettmann, 11, 30, 31, ©Cyril Ruoso/JH Editorial/Minden, 22; Dreamstime: Matthewbam, 38; Getty Images: Dr Clive Bromhall, 24, Duffy-Marie Arnoult/WireImage, 42, Giorgio Cosulich, 36, JENS SCHLUETER/AFP, 37, Manoj Shah, 13, Apic, front cover; Landov: CBS, 25; National Geographic: Hugo Van Lawick, 4, 16, 17, 19, 23, 26, 27, MICHAEL NICHOLS, 29, 33, 34, 35, ROBERT I.M. CAMPBELL, 18; Shutterstock: Ferenc Szelepcsenyi, 41, PHOTOCREO Michal Bednarek, 10, Sergey Uryadnikov, 5, Matt Tilghman, design element; © The Jane Goodall Institute: 6, 8, 9, 14, 20, 21, 32

We would like to thank Michael Bright for his invaluable help in the preparation of this book.

Every effort has been made to contact copyright holders of any material reproduced in this book. Any omissions will be rectified in subsequent printings if notice is given to the publisher.

007009CTPSF14

Contents

Some words are printed in bold, **like this**. You can find out
what they mean by looking in the glossary on page 45.

Who Is Jane Goodall?

As a young girl, Jane Goodall loved animals. From worms to chickens, from dogs to horses, she was interested in all animals and the way they behaved. As an adult, Goodall has used her passion for animals to change the world for the better.

Goodall is one of the best-known scientists in the world.

Goodall followed her life's dream by moving to Africa to study wild chimpanzees. At first, her methods of studying the animals attracted **criticism**. People could not understand why a young woman would venture into the forests of Africa by herself.

Other scientists faulted her for **humanizing** the animals by giving them names and believing they had emotions. Yet Goodall is now honored for her observations. And her methods have become the standard way to study animals in the wild.

From scientist to inspiration

Jane Goodall is one of the world's most easily recognizable scientists. She started off as a scientist who studied chimpanzees. Her research changed the way people think about chimps, the closest animal relative to humans. It also changed the way we think about ourselves as humans.

Chimpanzees have become extinct in a number of African nations.

However, her work and goals have changed over the years. Now, Goodall says that she is an **activist** first and foremost. Her goal is to make the world a better place. She does this by standing up for chimps and other animals that cannot speak for themselves. And she encourages young people to take charge and make things better. She says: "What you do makes a difference, and you have to decide what kind of difference you want to make."

What Was Goodall's Early Life Like?

Valerie Jane Goodall was born in London, England, on April 3, 1934. She was the first child of Mortimer Morris-Goodall and Margaret "Vanne" Joseph. Mortimer was an engineer and a top race car driver who traveled throughout Europe competing in races. Vanne was a housewife.

Jane and her stuffed pet, "Jubilee," were the best of friends.

Another important person in Jane's life was Nancy Sowden, whom she called "Nanny." Nanny came to live with the Goodalls when Jane was just three weeks old. Her job was to care for the new baby.

A love of animals

From an early age, Jane was fascinated with animals. All living creatures, big or small, furry or scaly, attracted her attention. One evening, Nanny was horrified to find that Jane had dug up a bunch of earthworms. She was keeping her new pets under her pillow!

Other pets soon followed. Jane had a tortoise named Johnny Walker and a dog named Peggy. At the age of two, she rode a horse for the first time. The one creature that Jane did not immediately love was her new baby sister, Judy, who was born on Jane's fourth birthday. But the two would later become very close.

DID YOU KNOW?

Jane's love of chimps may have been sparked by a stuffed animal. For her first birthday, Jane's father brought her a special toy. It was a stuffed chimpanzee, one of dozens created to celebrate the birth of the London Zoo's first chimp born in **captivity**. Jane loved "Jubilee," as she named it, and he quickly became her favorite toy. She still has him today.

World War II changes everything

In 1939 the lives of the Morris-Goodall family changed forever when England declared war on Germany, marking the start of **World War II**. Jane's father signed up to fight, and the rest of the family moved to Bournemouth, on the southern coast of England. Jane and Judy spent the rest of their childhoods there.

Although she was bright and inquisitive, Jane did not care much for school. She preferred reading books on her own. One of her favorite books was *The Story of Doctor Dolittle*. This book was about a man who could speak to and understand animals.

Jane was an intelligent child who was interested in learning all about animals.

DID YOU KNOW?

Jane performed her first scientific research project when she was just five years old. She knew that eggs came from hens, but she wanted to find out exactly how the process worked. So, she hid in the family's henhouse until she observed one of the chickens laying an egg.

Jane began riding horses at a young age and was a skilled rider.

A house full of women

World War II, which lasted until 1945, forever changed Jane's family. One of her uncles was killed in the fighting. Although her father survived the war, he and Jane's mother divorced soon after. Jane grew up in a house surrounded by strong women, including her mother, her aunts, and her grandmother. (Nanny had married and moved into a home of her own.)

Jane's tree

In Bournemouth, Jane's grandmother, whom she called "Danny," gave her a big, beautiful beech tree on her 10th birthday. Jane made her grandmother write up a will that promised that the tree would be hers forever.

Finding a way to Africa

After Goodall graduated from high school in 1952, she traveled to London. Here she took classes to become a secretary. She held jobs working at a clinic, a university, and a company that made **documentary films**. But Goodall yearned for more. She wanted to travel to Africa.

Goodall had been fascinated with Africa since she was a young child. She read everything she could about Africa's land and wildlife. In London, she visited museums and spent hours looking at the African exhibits. She took a job as a waitress back at home in Bournemouth and saved her earnings. Her goal was to save enough for a trip to Africa.

Goodall fell in love with the African landscape and soon called it home.

Louis Leakey and his wife Mary discovered important fossils at sites in Tanzania and Kenya.

The first trip

In 1955 a friend had asked Goodall to come visit her at her new home in Kenya, in Africa. In 1957 Goodall bought a ticket for a ship called the *Kenya Castle* and packed her bags. The trip along Africa's western and southern coastlines was thrilling for 22-year-old Goodall. While the rough seas made many of the passengers sick, she enjoyed every minute of the three-week trip.

Goodall fell in love with Africa. She decided that this would be her new home. After living in Kenya for a month, she met Louis Leakey. Leakey was a famous scientist in the fields of **archaeology** and **paleontology**. When Leakey offered the young woman a job, she said yes.

In her own words

In her book *My Life with the Chimpanzees*, Goodall describes keeping alive her dream of traveling to Africa. She said:

"Had I forgotten [my dream of Africa]? Absolutely not ... I continued to read books about animals, especially African animals ... Always I was waiting for my lucky break."

Why Did Goodall Study Chimpanzees?

At first Goodall worked for Dr. Leakey as his secretary. She had an office in a **natural history** museum in Kenya, which Leakey ran. Here she organized the scientist's research notes.

Goodall impressed Leakey with her knowledge of animals and with her curiosity. He soon became convinced that she was exactly the right person to carry out his next project. He wanted someone to spend 10 years in the wild studying chimpanzees, humankind's closest relative. When Goodall said she was interested in the project, Leakey told her, "I've been waiting for you to tell me that."

Goodall stayed in the African wild to research chimpanzees and their similarities to humans.

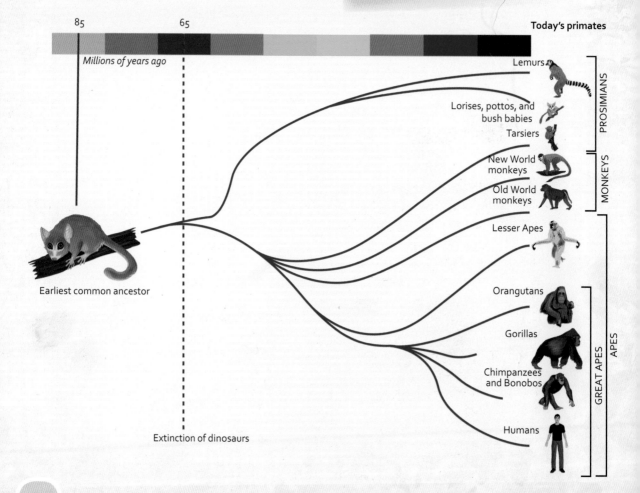

Millions of years ago

85   65

Today's primates

Lemurs

Lorises, pottos, and bush babies

Tarsiers

New World monkeys

Old World monkeys

Lesser Apes

Orangutans

Gorillas

Chimpanzees and Bonobos

Humans

Earliest common ancestor

Extinction of dinosaurs

PROSIMIANS

MONKEYS

APES

GREAT APES

Chimpanzees are **endangered** animals, with only about 300,000 in existence today.

But before Goodall could begin her research, Leakey needed to find funding for the project—and an escort for the young scientist. Many people were concerned about a young woman venturing into the forests alone to study chimps.

Louis Leakey

Louis S. B. Leakey was born in 1903 in Kenya, the son of British **missionaries**. When he was in college, he began hunting for **fossils** that might give him clues about the **evolution** of humans. For the rest of his life, he conducted digs and studied bones. Because apes are humans' closest relatives, he was also interested in learning more about humans by studying these **primates**.

DID YOU KNOW?

The following are some interesting facts about chimpanzees:

- Humans and chimps share as much as 98 percent of the same **DNA**.
- Chimps can grow to be 5 feet, 5 inches (170 centimeters) tall and weigh as much as 130 pounds (59 kilograms).
- Wild chimps usually live to be about 45 years old.
- Although chimps can walk upright, they prefer going around on all fours.
- Chimps sleep in "night nests" that they build in trees.

Founding a chimp research center

In July 1960, 26-year-old Goodall set out for the Gombe Stream Chimpanzee **Reserve** in what is now Tanzania. Her mother, Vanne, went along with her to help her set up the camp.

In her own words

Many people were not sure that Jane Goodall was the best choice for the chimp study. As a result, it was difficult to find money for the project. In a 2009 interview, Goodall recalled:

"Who was going to give money to a crazy project like a young girl straight from England, no degree, going out into a potentially dangerous situation?"

At first, the camp was made up of just two tents. One tent was for Goodall and her mother. The other was for the camp's cook. Few would have suspected that the camp would grow to become a world-class research center. Goodall would later rename her camp the Gombe Stream Research Center.

Goodall's mother, Vanne, was her first research partner.

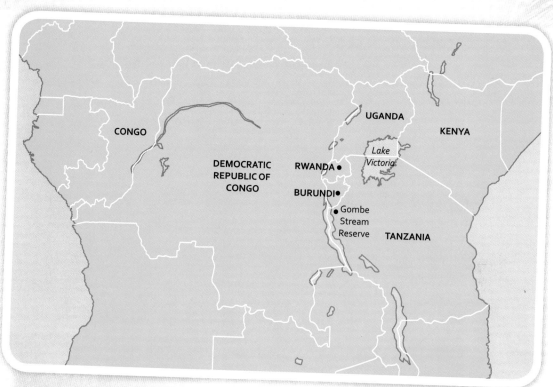

Goodall founded the Gombe Stream Research Center on the eastern shore of Lake Tanganyika in Tanzania.

Project goals

At Gombe, Goodall studied wild chimps living in their natural **habitat**. Although some people had studied chimpanzees in zoos and in laboratories, few people had done so in the wild. Those who had tried did not stay long. Chimps in the wild are difficult to approach and observe, and the work can be unrewarding.

Leakey wanted to better understand the way early humans had lived. He felt that the best way to do this was to study chimps. And Leakey knew that the study needed to be done soon: chimpanzees were—and are—an endangered species.

No easy task

Goodall went out to look for chimps to study as soon as her tent was set up. But she quickly discovered that observing the animals would not be an easy task. Although she saw two chimps on her first trek into the forest, the animals quickly fled when they caught sight of her.

For the first months of her research, Goodall spent most of her time observing the chimps from far away. The animals were still not used to her, and they would not allow her to get close. Goodall was frustrated and unhappy. But by watching the chimps through her binoculars, she learned about the different groups in the region.

David Greybeard, named for his white beard, enjoyed the bananas Goodall left out in the camp. Over time, his love of bananas led to a close connection to Goodall.

Soon, other chimps had joined the "Banana Club." The Banana Club's headquarters were at Goodall's tent at Gombe.

The "Banana Club"

Finally, Goodall's patience paid off. One of the larger chimps that she had been watching visited the camp when Goodall was away. It had examined her tent, leaving behind quite a mess. It had even taken some bananas that the cook had left for Goodall.

The next day, Goodall left more bananas out for the curious chimp. With the young woman watching, the animal that she called David Greybeard entered the camp and took the bananas. Over time, David Greybeard would approach Goodall to see if she had any fruit in her pocket. The other chimps watched, and soon they, too, were coming to the camp in search of bananas. Goodall called these chimps the "Banana Club."

David Greybeard

David Greybeard was the first chimp to make a connection with Goodall. During her time at Gombe, she got to know him well. She described him as a calm chimp who liked to keep out of trouble. But if he could not find any bananas in the camp, he would walk into Goodall's tent and tear through her things while looking for fruit.

What Was Life Like in Gombe?

During her years in Gombe, Goodall came to know and study about half of the reserve's 100 or so chimps. She learned that each chimp had its own unique personality—just like humans. She saw that they had emotions, like humans, and could experience joy and sorrow. When one young chimp's mother died, for example, he lost the will to live and died soon after her. Like humans, the chimps were social animals that lived in family groups. They hugged, kissed, and even patted each other on the back for comfort.

Instead of following scientific practice and numbering each chimp, Goodall chose to name the animals that she studied. Many of the names she chose were based on their personalities. She even named one chimp Olly, after her own aunt named Olive.

Dian Fossey was Leakey's gorilla researcher.

"Leakey's Angels"

One of Louis Leakey's dreams was to conduct studies of three great ape species, two in Africa and one in Asia. Between 1960 and 1971, Leakey found three women willing to do the research. Goodall studied chimpanzees. Dian Fossey studied mountain gorillas. And Biruté Galdikas focused on orangutans. The three women were sometimes called "Leakey's Angels."

Criticism of Goodall

Not everyone agreed with Goodall's methods. Scientists objected to her giving her research subjects names and becoming attached to them. They felt that Goodall was mistaken when she compared the chimps to humans.

Many also criticized Goodall's decision to offer fruit and other items to the animals. This action, critics charged, might actually be changing the chimps' behaviors.

Goodall never let the criticism bother her. She continued her work, carefully observing and taking notes about the animals she saw each day. During her first few years, Goodall took about 850 pages of notes.

Goodall came to know and deeply care for the chimps she watched each day.

Flo and her family

During her earliest years, Goodall developed a special relationship with a chimpanzee she named Flo. Flo was one of the first female chimps to show an interest in the scientist. The two met one day in 1961, when Flo came into Goodall's camp with David Greybeard. Flo's presence in the camp attracted more chimps for Goodall to study.

Flo was an older chimpanzee and an amazing mother. Goodall learned a great deal about chimp families from Flo and her children. She named Flo and her offspring the F Family. When naming the chimps, Goodall gave all of Flo's babies names that began with the letter *F*. They were called Faben, Figan, Fifi, Flint, and Flame.

Flo was a good mother who taught her children the skills they needed to survive.

In her own words

When Flo died in 1972, her **obituary** appeared in the *London Times* newspaper. Goodall wrote:

"It is true that [Flo's] life was worthwhile because it enriched human understanding. But even if no one had studied the chimpanzees at Gombe, Flo's life, rich and full of vigor and love, would still have had a meaning … in the pattern of things."

Flo was more than 40 years old when she died in 1972. Flint, unable to adjust to life without her, died just a month later. The rest of Flo's children went on to be high-ranking members of the chimpanzee group at Gombe. Flo's daughter Fifi, who died in 2004, was the last surviving chimp that Goodall studied.

Today, Fifi's children and grandchildren continue to thrive in the Gombe Reserve.

Flo was quite old when baby Flint was born, but she took good care of him.

What Did Goodall Learn from Chimps?

Although she came under fire for her "unscientific" methods, Goodall learned many things that had not previously been known about chimpanzees. One of the first things she learned was a big surprise: chimpanzees eat meat!

Until this time, most people thought that chimps were **vegetarians**. Vegetarians eat fruits, vegetables, and plants. But one day, Goodall watched David Greybeard and two other chimps eating a young bush pig. She later discovered that chimps would hunt and eat other small animals, including monkeys.

DID YOU KNOW?

Unlike her chimp friends, Jane Goodall is a vegetarian. In 2006 she wrote a book called *Harvest for Hope*. In it Goodall talks about how important she thinks it is to eat a healthy, plant-based diet and support local farmers. Goodall believes that it is one small thing that every person can do to make the world a better place.

Chimpanzees are omnivores. This means that they will eat all kinds of food, including plants, insects, and other animals.

Goodall kept careful track of the Gombe chimps.

The dark side of nature

Later Goodall made an even more shocking discovery. She found that, in some cases, chimps were cannibals. This means that they eat their own kind. During her time studying the Gombe chimps, she saw some of them kill and eat the babies of **rival** chimps.

Goodall would also eventually learn that, like humans, chimps wage war against each other. While studying at Gombe, she watched one group of chimps wage a four-year war against a second group. The war ended when most of the chimps in one of the groups had been killed. Goodall also observed male chimps battle and outsmart each other to try to be the leader of a group.

Rethinking the link

David Greybeard was behind a second important discovery that Goodall made during her early years at Gombe. She watched the chimp as he picked a blade of grass, then poked it into a termite hill. Then she saw David Greybeard eat the insects that clung to the grass. The chimp had used a tool!

Redefining man

When Leakey learned of Goodall's discovery that chimps used tools, he sent a telegram to Gombe. It said: "We shall now have to redefine tool, redefine man, or accept chimpanzees as humans." This is why Goodall is sometimes known as "the woman who redefined man."

Goodall found that chimps, like humans, can create and use tools.

Goodall was the first scientist to have such close contact with wild chimps

Until that moment, some experts had considered the use of tools to be the difference between humans and animals. Now, scientists had to rethink what being human meant. Today, the difference is said to be the use of a spoken language.

Back to England

Goodall's discoveries were exciting news. Now it would be easier for Leakey to get more funding to continue the chimpanzee project. But in order for Goodall to remain at Gombe, Leakey insisted that she first return to England. He had arranged for her to study at the University of Cambridge, as he wanted to make sure that other scientists took her seriously.

In 1961 Goodall left Gombe to begin her studies. The whole time she was at Cambridge, she worried that her chimp friends would forget her. She spent as little time at the college as possible. Whenever she could, she returned to visit the chimps at Gombe.

Success and fame

The National Geographic Society had helped pay for Goodall's project. The group was pleased with her discoveries. In August 1962, the society sent a photographer to Gombe to take photos and shoot film showing the young woman at work.

The photographer who traveled to Gombe was named Hugo van Lawick. He and Goodall had much in common, especially their love of animals. Van Lawick shot many photos of Goodall, and he later made a movie that Goodall thought was wonderful.

Hugo van Lawick

Hugo van Lawick was a Dutch **baron** and respected nature photographer when he first met Goodall. Born in Indonesia, he had begun photographing wild animals in Africa in 1959. Van Lawick won several awards over the years for his films about animals.

Goodall's first *National Geographic* cover brought her international attention.

Hugo van Lawick took hundreds of photos of Goodall and the Gombe chimps.

Changes for Goodall

In 1963 Goodall's first article for *National Geographic* magazine was published. The story received a great deal of attention and made her a well-known scientist around the world. But the article also led to something else. Goodall and Van Lawick had fallen in love.

On March 28, 1964, the pair married in London. Their honeymoon was cut short when they learned that Flo had given birth to a baby. Goodall and her new husband rushed back to Africa to see the new addition to the F Family. It was baby Flint.

In 1966 Goodall was awarded a **doctorate** in **ethology** from the University of Cambridge. Ethology is the study of animal behavior. Goodall is one of just eight people to earn such a degree without first receiving a standard college degree.

A "bush baby" is born

On March 4, 1967, Goodall and her husband welcomed a new addition to their own family group: a baby boy. Although they named the baby Hugo Eric Louis van Lawick, his mother and father called him "Grub."

Grub had an unusual childhood. Goodall tried many of the chimpanzee child-rearing methods she had seen Flo use. During his earliest years, he went along with his parents when they studied chimps, hyenas, and other animals. Grub grew up watching zebras, ostriches, lions, baboons, and other animals run wild.

Goodall knew, though, that the forest could be a dangerous place for little Grub. Chimpanzees and other animals might harm the baby while hunting for food. To make sure he was safe, Goodall built a special cage for Grub to play in. She never left him alone at Gombe.

Baby Grub watched his parents at work, studying Africa's wildlife.

Goodall has said that her most important mission was raising her son.

A new focus

Grub's birth did not stop Goodall's chimp project. But it did change the way she worked. Instead of following the chimps herself, she had students do this part of the job. In the morning, Goodall oversaw their efforts and wrote reports. In the afternoon, she taught Grub his lessons.

In 1970 Goodall published a picture book with photos by her husband. The book was called *Grub the Bush Baby*, and it introduced readers everywhere to her little boy.

Hugo Eric Louis "Grub" van Lawick

Grub is now a grown man with a family of his own. He lives in Tanzania with his wife and has three children. Like his mother, Grub loves animals. Recently, he worked on a project to save hippos living in one of Tanzania's national parks.

How Has Goodall Helped Chimps Around the World?

By 1972 about 100 people were living and working at the Gombe Stream Research Center. These people, Africans and students alike, helped Goodall with her research on the chimps. The early 1970s were also a time of personal change for Goodall. In 1974 she and her husband divorced.

The year after the divorce, four students were kidnapped by armed **guerilla** forces. They were held for ransom before finally being released. The violent raid on Gombe made it unsafe for Goodall and Grub to stay there anymore. In the coming years, she spent more time away from her chimps.

Goodall's youth and personality made her an appealing **advocate** for chimps and other animals.

Goodall's second husband, Derek Bryceson, speaks to voters to be re-elected as a member of parliament in Tanzania.

Derek Bryceson

In 1975, Goodall married her second husband, Derek Bryceson. Bryceson was a former British Royal Air Force pilot who had been seriously injured during World War II. When Goodall met him, he was a member of Tanzania's parliament (law-making group) and served as director of the country's national parks. The pair was married until Bryceson's death in 1980.

In her own words

When Goodall gave medicine to sick chimps, she was criticized for not allowing nature to take its course. She later wrote:

"It seems to me ... that humans have already interfered to such a major extent, usually in a very *negative* way ... with so many animals in so many places that a certain amount of positive interference is desirable."

Goodall put the time away to good use. In 1977 she founded the Jane Goodall Institute for Wildlife Research, Education, and Conservation. In the coming years, the organization would work to raise funds and protect great apes and other endangered animals around the world. She also gave talks about the studies that were still taking place at Gombe.

A new focus

In the 1980s, Goodall spent less and less time at Gombe. Instead, she focused on running and expanding the organization she had founded. In the coming years, Goodall turned her attention to chimps throughout Africa. She chose to use the respect and fame she had earned at Gombe to become an advocate for all wild chimpanzees.

Goodall learned that chimps in the Congo were in particular danger. There, adult chimps were illegally hunted and killed for **bush meat**. Bush meat is the meat from wild animals that is sold in some parts of the world. It can come from elephants, antelopes, crocodiles, bush pigs—and chimpanzees. Adult chimps are killed for their meat, but the smaller ones are often sold as pets.

Goodall plants a tree with the help of students in Tanzania.

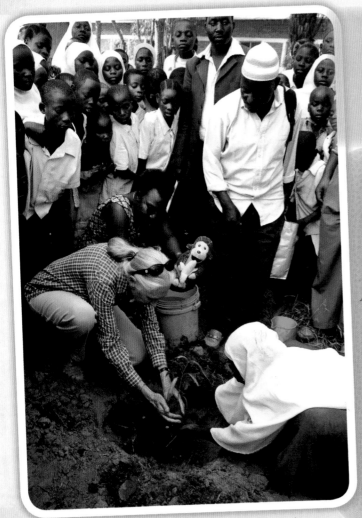

The TACARE program

A key part of protecting wild chimps is educating people who live near them so that they understand the chimps' importance. In 1994 Goodall founded the TACARE program. Through the program, men and women living near wild chimp groups learn how to earn livings by protecting the chimps and their habitats. Then they can give up old activities, such as cutting down forests and hunting for bush meat.

A safe place for rescued chimps

Goodall took action. In 1992 she helped found Tchimpounga in the Congo. This sanctuary takes in young chimps that were left alone when their parents were killed by hunters. The **sanctuary** gives rescued chimps care, attention, and a safe place to live for the rest of their lives.

Over the years, the number of rescued chimps at Tchimpounga has grown. Recently, the sanctuary was improved and expanded, with three new islands added to make room for all of the animals. The makeover was funded by Goodall's organization.

About 150 rescued chimps make their home at Tchimpounga.

Helping chimpanzees in captivity

Goodall also works to ensure that chimps held in captivity are treated with care and dignity. She became concerned about this issue when she heard animal rights activists speaking about the condition of chimps that live in laboratories. She began visiting labs and research centers to see the situation for herself.

The United States is one of the few countries that continues to use chimps for medical research. More than 900 of these intelligent animals are kept in laboratories for this purpose. Those who work with these chimps say that the animals can provide valuable information to scientists and researchers. The information could be used to improve the lives of humans with deadly diseases.

Goodall inspects a laboratory to see how the chimps there are treated.

Goodall understands the importance of the research. But she wants the captive chimps to be treated better. She has worked with laboratories and research centers to improve living conditions for the animals. She has also written to the U.S. Congress to ask that certain types of medical testing on captive chimps end immediately.

Meeting JoJo

Goodall met JoJo the chimpanzee in 1988. He was being kept in a laboratory for tests on **HIV** and **AIDS**. The big chimp was kept in a small cage with thick bars. He was isolated, unable to see others of his own kind. Goodall and JoJo developed an immediate bond. When Goodall began to cry, JoJo wiped her tears away.

In her own words

Goodall's meeting with JoJo was emotional. She later wrote:

"Could he remember that life [in Africa]? ... Did he sometimes dream of the great trees with the breeze rustling through the canopy, the birds singing, the comfort of his mother's arms?...There was no comfort for him of soft forest floor or leafy nest high in the treetops."

Goodall and JoJo developed an instant bond the first time they met.

Investigating zoos

At first Goodall believed that chimps should not be held in captivity at all. She believed that chimps were better off in the wild than in laboratories or zoos. She also campaigned to stop the use of chimps in entertainment.

But over the years, Goodall's beliefs have shifted. Recently, she has said that some animals are better off in good zoos. This change in position has caused controversy. It also caused her to split from Advocates for Animals, a group that she had worked with for many years. This group believes that no animals should be kept in zoos.

Goodall believes that some animals may live better lives in good zoos.

ChimpanZoo

In 1984 Goodall founded a special research group called ChimpanZoo. The program's goal was to study the health and behavior of chimpanzees that are held in captivity in zoos and other places. The group also helped improve the lives of captive chimps by working with and educating their keepers.

Today Goodall travels to zoos throughout the world. She speaks with zookeepers and others who can make a difference in the lives of animals held in captivity. Goodall wants to make sure that chimps everywhere are treated with kindness, dignity, and respect.

Goodall's goal is to make sure that chimps held in captivity have rich and rewarding lives.

What Is Goodall Up to Today?

Jane Goodall has led a very busy and rewarding life. Over the years, she has received more than 60 awards for her work to save chimps and other animals. One major honor was given to her in 2002. That year, she was named a **United Nations** (UN) Messenger of Peace. In this role, she helps focus worldwide attention on UN efforts to improve the lives of people throughout the world.

In 2013 Goodall was the grand marshal of the Tournament of Roses parade in California. A grand marshal is a special, honorary position in a parade that is awarded to famous or important people.

Goodall's outstanding life work was also recognized by the queen of England. In 2004 Queen Elizabeth II made Goodall a dame commander of the Order of the British Empire. This honorary title is considered a great achievement. Goodall received the honor for her services to the environment.

Jane Goodall, screen star

Goodall has been the subject—and star—of many films. One of the most recent movies, called *Jane's Journey*, was released in 2010. This documentary shows Goodall's journey, from being a young girl who loved animals to becoming a strong woman who continues to change the world. Her friends and family also appear in the movie.

Over the years, Goodall has written a number of books, both for adults and children. Of course, many other people have also written books about the scientist and her important work.

In her own words

On her organization's website, Goodall says:

"I encourage young people around the world, boys and girls, to follow their dreams, whether they dream of a career in the arts, academia, business or science. My mother always told me that if I really wanted something, I should never give up, and I would find a way. And she was right!"

A busy schedule

Goodall continues to work hard to save chimps and to create a better world. She is still writing. Her most recent book was published in 2013. She is also still traveling to universities, zoos, and other places to give lectures. Over the years, Goodall has inspired millions of listeners.

Goodall still keeps a demanding schedule. In fact, she works about 300 days of the year! In a recent interview, Goodall said that she had not stayed in one place for more than three weeks since 1986.

Goodall says that the next part of her life will be devoted to actively trying to save the environment—and all the creatures in it. When she talks to people about chimps and other issues, she tells them that the most important thing they can do is to be active and do something—even a very small thing—to change things for the better.

DID YOU KNOW?

In 1991 Goodall and a group of Tanzanian children founded Roots and Shoots. This group works to involve young people in caring about chimps and other endangered animals. Over the years, the program has grown to 131 countries and thousands of volunteers. Goodall says that inspiring children to be the caretakers of our environment is the cause that is closest to her heart.

In her own words

In an interview, Goodall was asked why, at her age, she continues to keep such a busy schedule. She replied:

"Because there's less of my life left and so much to do."

Today she travels to Gombe about twice a year. Her favorite place on Earth, Gombe allows Goodall to "recharge her batteries."

Jane Goodall continues to work tirelessly to make Earth a better place.

What Impact Has Goodall's Work Had on Animal Conservation?

When a young Jane Goodall arrived at the Gombe Reserve in 1960, she had little idea how important her research would be. Goodall's methods of researching made scientists rethink how they studied animals in the wild. Her discoveries about chimp behavior revolutionized the way people around the world thought about chimps—and about humans.

Over the years, thousands of children from around the world have joined Roots and Shoots.

As a result, many other people around the world now work hard to save chimpanzees. In the United States and Canada, groups are working to remove chimps from testing facilities and roadside circuses and to place them in sanctuaries and zoos. One of the largest chimp sanctuaries is Save the Chimps in Fort Pierce, Florida. It is home to nearly 300 rescued chimpanzees, and it is not open to the public.

Who will save the chimps?

Despite these and other efforts, the population of chimps in the wild continues to decline. In Africa, the loss of their natural habitat is taking the deadliest toll. Today chimpanzees have gone extinct (died out) in four African countries.

Chimp advocates say that stronger laws must be passed and new preserves must be created to help the animals. Goodall says that to save chimps and other endangered animals, people everywhere must stop asking, "How will this affect me now?" Instead, we must ask, "How will this affect my people in the future?"

In her own words

Goodall feels that children hold the key to a healthy future. She has said:

"Hundreds and thousands of young people around the world can break through and can make this a better world... The message is that every one of us makes a difference every day, that we can't live through a day without impacting the world... Understanding, spending time learning about and thinking about the consequences [results] of the little choices we make each day, and how they will affect the environment, how they will affect animals and the human community."

Timeline

1934 Valerie Jane Goodall is born in London, England, on April 3

1939 World War II begins, and Goodall's father signs up to fight for England

1952 Goodall graduates from high school and moves to London

1957 Travels by ship to Africa

1960 Arrives at the Gombe Stream Chimpanzee Reserve with her mother, Vanne

1961 Makes several groundbreaking discoveries about chimpanzee behavior; leaves Gombe to begin studying at the University of Cambridge in England

1963 *National Geographic* magazine publishes Goodall's first article about her chimp research

1964 Goodall marries Hugo van Lawick in London

1966 Goodall earns her doctorate in ethology. The Gombe Stream Research Center is founded

1967 On March 4, Hugo Eric Louis van Lawick is born. His family nicknames him "Grub"

1974 Goodall and van Lawick divorce

1975 Goodall marries her second husband, Derek Bryceson

1977 The Jane Goodall Institute for Wildlife Research, Education, and Conservation is founded

1984 The ChimpanZoo is founded

1986 Goodall decides to focus her attention on chimps around the world, both wild and in captivity

1988 Meets JoJo, the captive chimp

1991 Roots and Shoots is founded

1992 The chimp sanctuary Tchimpounga is founded to care for rescued chimpanzees

1994 Goodall creates TACARE to involve local people in saving chimps and their environment

2002 The United Nations names Goodall a Messenger of Peace

2004 Goodall is made a dame commander of the Order of the British Empire by Queen Elizabeth II

2010 *Jane's Journey*, a documentary about Goodall, is released

2013 Goodall publishes *Seeds of Hope: Wisdom and Wonder from the World of Plants*

Glossary

activist person who takes direct action to try to solve a problem or to change a bad situation

advocate person who supports or works for a cause

AIDS short for "acquired immunodeficiency syndrome," a deadly disease caused by a virus that harms a body's ability to fight other diseases

archaeology study of ancient people and the way they lived

baron nobleman; person from a high-ranking family

bush meat meat from wild animals that is eaten or sold for food

captivity being held in confinement; not free

criticism negative remarks about something

DNA short for "deoxyribonucleic acid," a substance that is found in all living things and carries the information about how each thing will look and function

doctorate highest degree given by colleges and universities

documentary film movie that describes actual events in a factual way

endangered at risk of dying out

ethology study of animal behavior

evolution process through which living creatures gradually change to a more complex form over a long period of time

fossil remains or impression of a living thing from long ago

great ape large primate, including the chimpanzee, gorilla, and orangutan

guerilla member of a group of independent fighters who use unconventional fighting methods

habitat place where an animal makes its home

HIV short for "human immunodeficiency virus," a virus that causes AIDS

humanize assign human-like qualities to an animal

missionary person who spreads his or her religion to other areas

natural history study of living things

obituary newspaper notice that reports the death of a person or animal

paleontology science of learning more about ancient times through finding and studying fossil remains

population number of a type of animal or people that live in an area

primate group of animals that includes humans, apes, monkeys, and lemurs

reserve land that is set aside for a special purpose

rival opponent; enemy

sanctuary safe place to live

species group of living things that are related to each other

United Nations organization, headquarted in New York City, that promotes world peace and equality

vegetarian animal or person that eats only plant-based foods

vervet monkey small, long-tailed African monkey

World War II war that took place from 1939 to 1945 and involved the world's most powerful nations

Find Out More

Books

Goodall, Jane. *Jane Goodall: 50 Years at Gombe: A Tribute to Five Decades of Wildlife Research, Education, and Conservation*. New York: Stewart, Tabori & Chang, 2010.

Malnor, Carol. *Champions of Wild Animals* (Earth Heroes). Nevada City, Calif.: Dawn Publications, 2010.

Moore, Heidi. *Chimpanzees* (Living in the Wild). Chicago: Heinemann Library, 2012.

Ottaviani, Jim, and Maris Wicks. *Primates: The Fearless Science of Jane Goodall, Dian Fossey, and Biruté Galdikas*. New York: First Second, 2013.

Spilsbury, Richard, and Louise Spilsbury. *Chimpanzee Troops* (Animal Armies). New York: PowerKids, 2013.

Websites

www.centerforgreatapes.org
This website is devoted to protecting all great apes, including chimps, gorillas, and orangutans.

gombechimpanzees.org
Explore the website of the Jane Goodall Institute Research Center.

www.janegoodall.org
This is the website of Goodall's organization, the Jane Goodall Institute. Check in to see what Goodall is up to now!

ngm.nationalgeographic.com/1963/08/jane-goodall/goodall-text/1
Read the National Geographic story that started it all.

DVDs

Jane Goodall. New York: CBS Broadcasting, 2010.

Jane Goodall: My Life with Chimpanzees. Washington, D.C.: National Geographic Video, 2010.

Jane's Journey. New York: First Run Features, 2011

Places to Visit
Kansas City Zoo
6800 Zoo Drive
Kansas City, Missouri 64132
www.kansascityzoo.org
Named one of the best zoos in the United States, the Kansas City Zoo has been praised by Goodall for having an outstanding chimpanzee exhibit.

Travel with the Jane Goodall Institute
Goodall's organization offers trips to Tchimpounga in Africa or other locations around the world. Visit www.janegoodall.org/volunteer to learn more.

What can I do?
What part of Jane Goodall's journey inspired you? Can you think of ways that you might follow in Goodall's footsteps and help the world? If you are interested in the plight of chimpanzees, you might want to get together with your friends and look into Goodall's Roots and Shoots organization for young people. You can visit the website (rootsandshoots.org) for more information. You could also fund-raise to become a "chimp guardian" to an orphaned chimpanzee. Check out Goodall's website for more information.

Index